# I want to learn al-Fatihah

Written by Umm Bilaal Bint Sabir
Content Review @utrujjah_press
Cover Formatting @ilm.cards
Proofreading Umm AbdurRahmaan S. Bint Ahmed and Umm Yusuf
Typesetting and Design by Umm Bilaal Bint Sabir

2023 Al Huroof Publishing
© alhuroof
First Published December 2023
Second Edition April 2024

**ISBN 978-1-917065-11-5**

All rights reserved. No part of this publication may be reproduced stored in a retrieval system or transmitted in any form or by any means electronic, mechanical, photocopying, recording or otherwise without the prior written permission of the author.
All enquiries to: alhuroof@hotmail.com
@al.huroof

Al Huroof Publishing

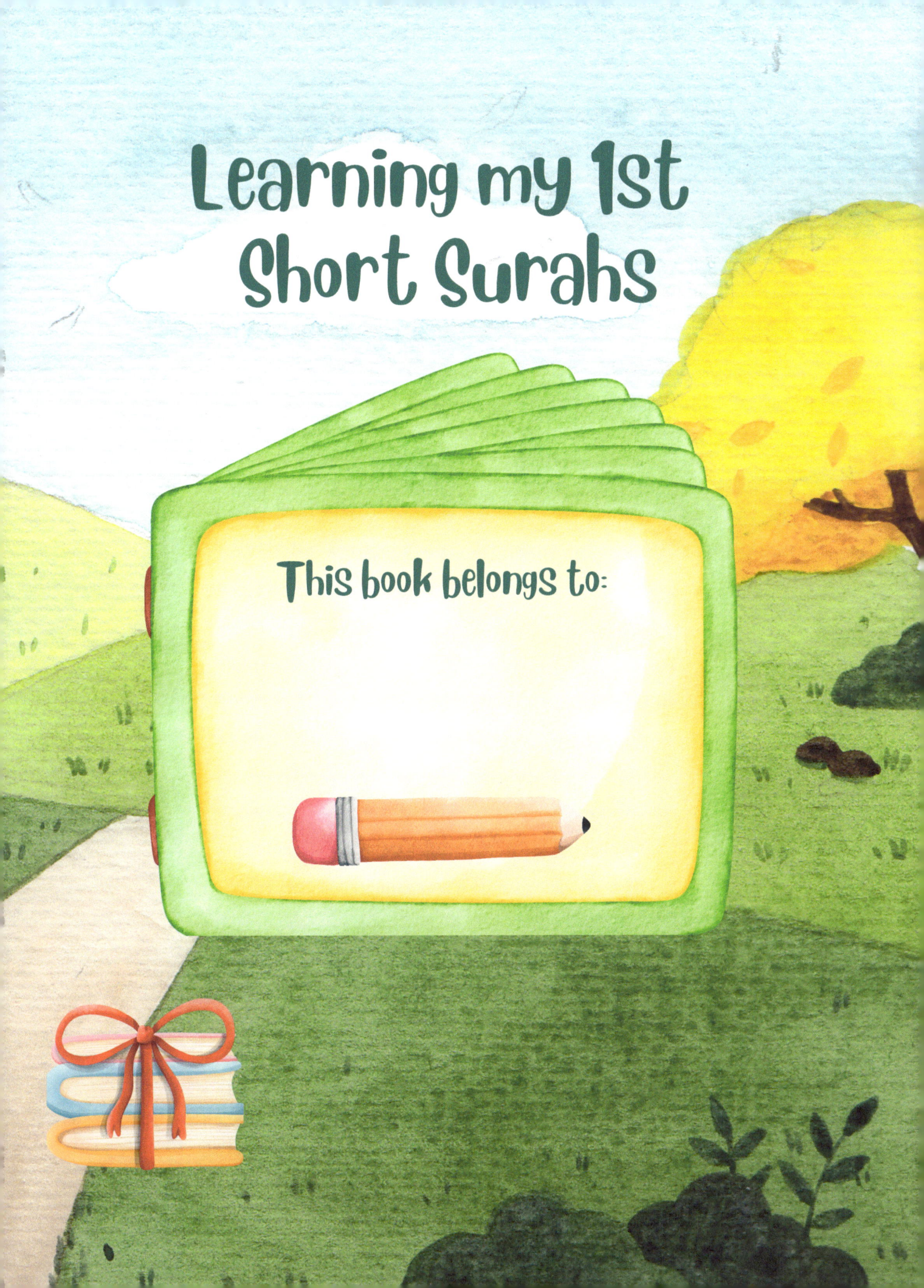

**All Praise is for Allaah the Lord of the whole of creation and may Allaah extol and grant peace and security to our Prophet Muhammad (sallAllaahu 'alayhi wa sallam), and to his true followers and to his companions (radhiAllaahu 'anhum), all of them. To Proceed:**

## How to Use this Book

Learning to read Surah al-Fatihah is a special time for any young Muslim who is beginning their journey of memorising the Qur'aan.

Learning, memorising and understanding the Qur'aan can be difficult all at once. Understanding the meaning can be even more difficult for non-Arab speakers, especially if they do not know the Arabic language.

This book has been designed as a helping guide for English Speakers who would like to understand the meaning of the English translation of Surah Al-Fatihah as they are learning it. A word for word translation of the meaning* has been given followed by a whole verse (ayah). There will be a natural difference with the single word and when the whole ayah is read together. This has been taken from the explanation (tafseer) of the ayah. *The Qur'aan cannot be translated only the meaning can be translated.

## References

The translation has been taken from The Noble Qur'aan, Darussalaam by Dr. Muhammad Hilali and Dr.Muhsin Khan. The tafseer of this Surah has been taken from the author's notes made from the tafseer of Surah al-Fatihah by Imaam as Saa'di rahimahullaah and explained by Shaykh Fawzaan hafidhahullaah.

## About Al Huroof

Al Huroof is a small project aimed at producing authentic Islamic teaching aids and material. These are based on the Qur'aan and Sunnah, with the understanding of the Prophet Muhammad (sallAllaahu 'alayhi wa sallam), and his righteous companions - Salaf-us-Saalih - (radhiAllaahu 'anhum). After thanking Allaah, Subhaanahu, we would like to thank all those who have aided in this book, from formatting, checking and feedback.

May Allaah accept it as sadaqa jaariyah from us, ameen.

I want to learn

# Surah al-Fatihah

How do I start?

# Let's go over some basic Arabic vowels that you will need for this surah.

Each ayah (verse) has been divided word by word. When you see this little sign it means 'Iqra' (read or recite).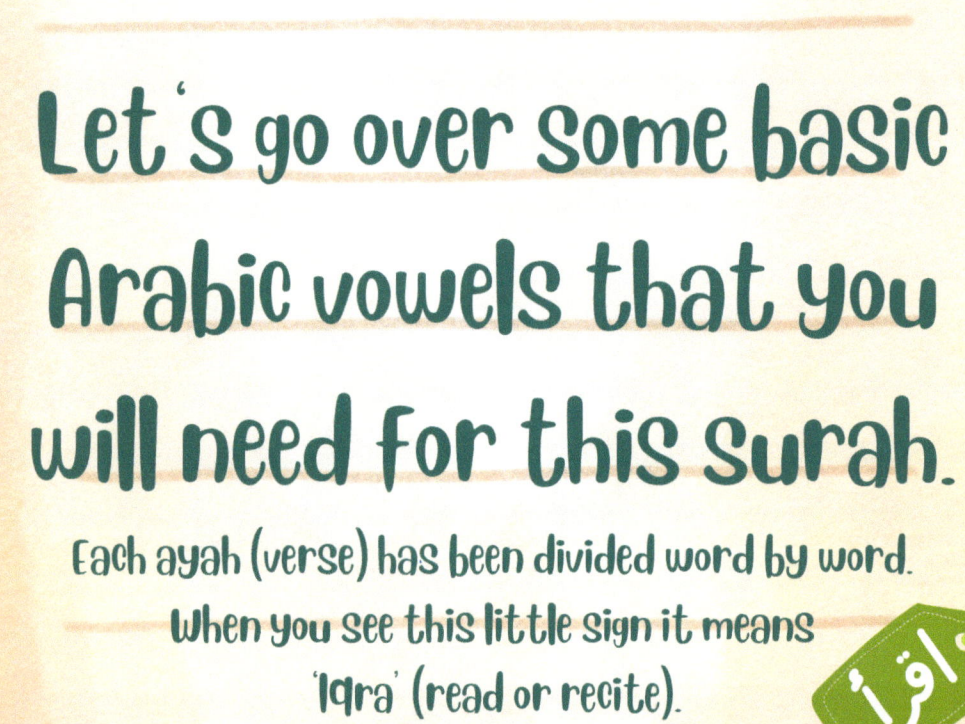

\*The tafseer of this surah has been taken from the works of Imaam as Saa'di rahimahullaah and explained by Shaykh Fawzaan hafidhahullah.

# Basic Vowels

### Dhamma

tu  bu  'u

### Kasrah

ti  bi  ii

### Fathah
أَ بَ تَ
ta  ba  a

### Shaddah

ab-bu  ab-bi  ab-ba

### Sukoon
أُبْ  إِبْ  أَبْ
ub  ib  ab

### Dhammatayn

bunn  unn

### Kasrahtayn

binn  inn

### Fatahtayn

bann  ann

### Lam - alif

laa

### Hamza-alif

'u  'i  'a

### Madd

4 or 6 counts

### Dagger Alif

This is a long 'a' sound

### Hamza-tul Wasl

This sound is not said if connecting with a previous word.

## In the name of Allaah

We say Bismillaah before we recite the Qur'aan. We also say it before we do something so that we can get Allaah's help and blessings in what we do. Saying Bismillaah also means we are calling upon all the names of Allaah.

# The Most Merciful

This is one of the beautiful names of Allaah. It means 'Rahma' which is mercy.

Allaah has a vast amount of Mercy and is the Most Merciful to all of His creation. We receive His Mercy everyday in so many ways.

# The Ever-Merciful

This is another one of the beautiful names of Allaah.

It means He is more Merciful, and gives special Mercy to those who believe in Him. Those who follow His Prophets and His Messengers and are Muslims.

# now say it together

In the name of Allaah,
The Most Merciful,
The Ever-Merciful.

## All Praises

This means that all praise is for Allaah alone. Allaah deserves to be praised because He is Perfect in every way: in His Names and Attributes and His Actions.

Allaah created and guided us and provides for us. It is part of Tawheed 'al Uloohiyyah'* to praise Him.

*(to single out Allaah for worship)

## be to Allaah

The name 'Allaah' is one of the greatest names of Allaah. Allaah has more than 99 Names and Attributes that we know of. There is a hadeeth that mentions 99 Names, and if you memorise them there is a great reward.

The name Allaah is Unique because it includes all the names of Allaah.

# Lord of

Rabb – means Lord.

Allaah is our Lord who created everything alone.

He provides, controls and protects for the whole creation alone.

This is Tawheed 'ar Ruboobiyyah* because Allaah is the Creator of Everything.

*(to single out Allaah for Lordship)

# the worlds
## (and everything that exists)

This means Allaah created the worlds, universe, heavens and everything between them.

This also includes the world of the humans, the world of the jinn, the world of animals, and everything we can or can't see in creation.

## now say it together

All Praises
be to Allaah,
Lord of the worlds,
(and everything that exists).

# The Most Merciful

Can you remember the meaning of this name? It is Allaah's 'Rahma' - Mercy that is for the entire creation! Allaah created mercy in 100 parts.

Allaah kept 99 parts to Himself and sent 1 part (to the Earth), for the creation.

# The Ever-Merciful

Allaah is especially Merciful to the believers.

The Prophet Muhammad (sallAllaahu 'alayhi wa sallam), said that the believers will receive the other 99 parts (of Mercy) on the Day of Judgement and in Paradise.*

*Sahih al Bukhari Book of Manners No 6000 and Muslim 2752

## now say it together

**The Most Merciful, The Ever-Merciful.**

# The Only Owner (and Only Judge) of

Maalik is one of the Names of Allaah. It means Allaah is the Owner of everything and everyday - especially the Day of Judgement.

Only Allaah will have the power and control on that Day because He is the true Master and King.

# (of) The Day of

The Day of Judgement is when everyone who has ever lived from the beginning of time to the end of time will be gathered together.

# Judgement

This means the account (hisaab) and reward (jazaa') that will take place on the Day of Judgement.

Everyone will be given the reward of what they used to do of their good or bad actions.

# الدِّينِ

## now say it together

The Only Owner (and the Only Judge) of the Day of Judgement.

# You Alone

We single out
Allaah alone
(for worship).

## We Worship

We only worship Allaah alone - not anyone or anything else. Worship is everything we do that Allaah is pleased with and we hope to get reward for. This includes: prayer, fasting, giving charity making du'aa and much more.

# and You Alone

We single out
Allaah alone
(when we ask)
for help.

# we ask for help

When we need help or guidance for something we should ask Allaah first.

Asking Allaah for help is also part of worship. He is the only One who can really help us.

## now say it together

You alone we worship and You alone we ask for help.

## guide us to

When we ask Allaah to guide us we are asking Him to guide us to the path of truth (Islam) and then to accept it.

After that we ask Allaah to keep us in this path and be successful in it.

# the path

This means the path of truth - Islam, the path of the Qur'aan and the path of following the Prophet Muhammad (sallAllaahu 'alayhi wa sallam).

## the straight

This is a straight path that is not crooked. If we are guided to the straight path we will never go astray. This is the path of Allaah, and the Sunnah of the Prophet (sallAllaahu 'alayhi wa sallam) and his companions (radiAllaahu 'anhum).

now say it together

Guide us to the Straight Path.

اهْدِنَا الصِّرَاطَ الْمُسْتَقِيمَ

اقْرَأ

# The Path

This is the path to Allaah that the Prophets ('alayhimus-salaam), the truthful, the people who die in the way of Allaah, the scholars and the righteous people follow.*

Surah An-Nisa ayah 176

## of those (people)

These are righteous people who Allaah is pleased with.

# You have blessed

The greatest blessings of Allaah is that He has guided people to His straight path, as well as so many other blessings from Him.

# (on) them

There are four types of people that Allaah is pleased with: the Prophets and Messengers ('alayhimus-salaam), the truthful, the people who call to Tawheed and the righteous people.*

Surah An-Nisa ayah 176

## now say it together

The path of those that You have blessed.

صِرَاطَ الَّذِينَ أَنْعَمْتَ عَلَيْهِمْ

# not (the way)

There are two groups of people that Allaah warns us about. This is the first group of people we should not be like.

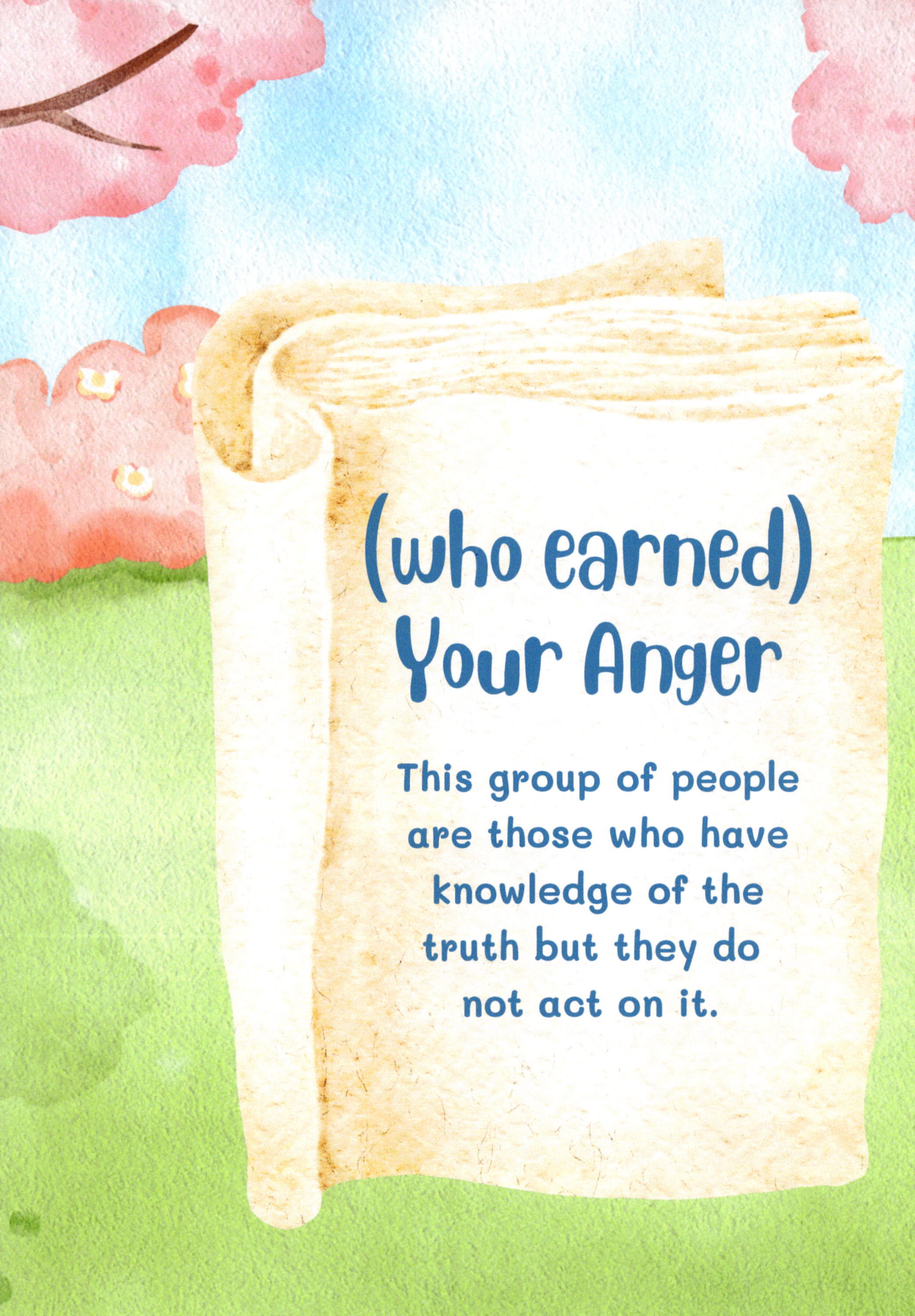

# (who earned) Your Anger

This group of people are those who have knowledge of the truth but they do not act on it.

# on them

This is why the Anger of Allaah is on them - because they have knowledge of the truth but they do not act on it.

# and not (of those)

Allaah warns us not to be like the second group of people (who are astray).

## who went astray

This group went astray because they do actions - without true and correct knowledge.

## now say it together

Not (the way) of those who earned Your Anger and not of those who went astray.

When you are ready you can try and recite the whole surah!

## الفاتحة

بِسْمِ ٱللَّهِ ٱلرَّحْمَٰنِ ٱلرَّحِيمِ

In the name of Allaah the Most Merciful, The ever-Merciful

ٱلْحَمْدُ لِلَّهِ رَبِّ ٱلْعَٰلَمِينَ

All praises be to Allaah Lord of the worlds, (heavens and all that is between them).

ٱلرَّحْمَٰنِ ٱلرَّحِيمِ

The Most Merciful, The Ever-Merciful.

مَٰلِكِ يَوْمِ ٱلدِّينِ

The Only Owner and the Only Judge of the Day of Judgement.

إِيَّاكَ نَعْبُدُ وَإِيَّاكَ نَسْتَعِينُ

You Alone we worship, You Alone we ask for help.

ٱهْدِنَا ٱلصِّرَٰطَ ٱلْمُسْتَقِيمَ

Guide us to the Straight Path.

صِرَٰطَ ٱلَّذِينَ أَنْعَمْتَ عَلَيْهِمْ

The path of those that You have blessed.

غَيْرِ ٱلْمَغْضُوبِ عَلَيْهِمْ وَلَا ٱلضَّآلِّينَ

Not (the way) of those who earned Your Anger and not of those who went astray.

www.ingramcontent.com/pod-product-compliance
Lightning Source LLC
Chambersburg PA
CBHW040054160426
43192CB00002B/66